MUDDLES

Juliana Daniels

authorHOUSE®

AuthorHouse™ UK
1663 Liberty Drive
Bloomington, IN 47403 USA
www.authorhouse.co.uk
Phone: 0800 047 8203 (Domestic TFN)
*   +44 1908 723714 (International)*

Published by AuthorHouse 12/16/2019

ISBN: 978-1-7283-9179-3 (sc)
ISBN: 978-1-7283-9178-6 (e)

Print information available on the last page.

This book is printed on acid-free paper.

**Dedicated to my husband
Philip and my son Kuuku**

My sincere gratitude goes to the Dean of Creative Arts, Dr Patrique De-Graft Yankson and the entire Faculty of Creative Arts of the University of Education, Winneba for the provision of the book cover image. I also appreciate Mr Richard Bampoe-Addo and Mr Enerst Abechie and Mr Godfred Nortey of the Department of English Education of the University of Education, Winneba for their editorial support. My final appreciation is to Miss Annie Robertson of the Centre for Audiology, UEW for her secretarial services. God richly bless you all for your dedication.

THE CHARACTERS

BAABA: Wife of Kobina Esan

KOBINA ESAN: Husband of Baaba

KUKUA: Baaba's younger sister

BADUA: Baaba's mother

TESSA: Baaba's bosom friend

ODUM: SRC President

NAANA: Baaba's friend

DR. JAY: Lecturer and Academic Counsellor

PROF. MANU: Lecturer

HON. AMPONSAH: Member of Parliament

REV. FR. MENSAH: Baaba's elder brother

EBUSUAPANYIN

LINGUIST

SPOKESPERSON

SYNOPSIS

BAABA: Baaba is a beautiful young woman of twenty-nine years with two children. She is married to Kobina Esan a middle school certificate holder currently trading in second-hand car parts at Abose Okine, a suburb in Accra. As a well-informed woman, with unspoken confusions that rule her thoughts, marriage to Kobina is the last thing she wanted but for her father's insistence. Therefore, gaining admission to the university also meant an opportunity to escape from what she deemed marital enslavement. On campus, she treads the dangerous path by dating one man after the other when she gains residential accommodation and begins to fraternize with her new society of freedom. This results in the dissolution of her marriage with Esan. At the end of her studies,

Baaba divorces Esan and later marries Saani. The couple relocates to America where they get married and have some more children.

ACT 1

SCENE I

(In the kitchen of Badua. She is frying kaakrow (mashed ripe plantain). Kukua, Baaba's younger sister is washing the dishes in the kitchen. Kukua and Badua in a conversation)

KUKUA: Mama, do you think Dada is getting better?

BADUA: Yes! Why do you ask?

KUKUA: I heard him coughing badly last night.

BADUA: *(sighing)* hmm! He had a difficult night. I haven't had a single sleep since that horrifying cough started. Your father is really in pain.

KUKUA: And what exactly did the doctors say is the problem?

BADUA: My daughter, now you are a woman. The university is a big place. When your results come in and they are good, you would go to school. That is where you have to be careful with what you do with your life.

KUKUA: Mama, you just said I am a woman now. I guess that also means that you know I know that what you just said is not an answer to the question I asked you.

BADUA: It is my daughter. It only requires you to begin to think like a woman.

KUKUA: Does womanhood come with speaking in parables when you can simply state your answer in plain language?

BADUA: Not necessarily womanhood. Womanhood comes with maturity and maturity comes with speaking and understanding in parables.

KUKUA: Are you then implying that I don't understand because I am not matured?

BADUA: Maybe, but I don't believe that you don't understand. I think you do not know that you understand. However, you should never forget what I just told you. Out there, you will be on your own and there you must survive. You only need a little more time to be able to wash your hands well so that you can dine with the elders.

KUKUA: I understand you on this one, Mama. I even think Baaba needs this advice more than I do.

BADUA: What makes you think so?

KUKUA: Well, she is the one going to university this year, in fact only next month.

BADUA: So?

KUKUA: You should have a real talk with her before she leaves.

BADUA: You are right and I agree with you. Your sister is going through so much. Life has not been easy for her. But I have faith in her. She is a strong woman and that will see her through. I know she knows what to do out there. I trust her to make the right decisions. She has managed her affairs fairly well so far. Going to university is a good decision. She needs the space to clear her head and take a second look at her life. She will be fine. St. Jude will continue to keep her.

(The sound of a cough runs through the kitchen) That should be your father again. Run, run, go and check on him while I take this *kaakrow* out of the hot oil. *(Kukua hurries out of the kitchen. Badua collects the fairly cooked mashed ripe plantain balls out of the hot palm oil, puts them in a strainer to drain the oil).*

ACT 1

SCENE 2

BAABA: Hmmm! This house smells good. Where is everybody? *(entering the kitchen, serves some kaakrow on a plate and adds some boiled red beans stew from a pot and leaves the kitchen shouting)* Where is everybody? Mama, Kukua,

BADUA: *(emerging from Dada's room she snaps)* shhhhhhhhhh! You like that. Why are you shouting out everybody's name like that? Must you let the evil people who seek us know where we are?

BAABA: Ooooohoo Mama! What evil spirits? Don't you go to church? Are you not a member of the Legions of Mary, Knights of St. John, Christian Mothers and what else, ehh St. Anthony's Guild etc.? How can you be afraid of evil spirits when you are also the prayer warriors' president for National St. Theresa's Women Society in the almighty Catholic Church? You see, that is why I say quit all these societies and be non-aligned like me. *(laughs)* Hahaaah!

BADUA: You make light of heavy matters my daughter. Where would you all have been but for my prayers and commitment to all these societies? You don't go to church and you don't pray and so as a mother, I have to be spiritually strong in order to intercede for you and the rest of the family.

BAABA: Yes Mama *(laughing, hugs her mother leading her to the sitting room)* Please sit down for me.

BADUA: *(Taking a seat, speaking in a low tone)* Take a seat too my daughter. How are you doing my dear?

BAABA: Very well, Mama. I am fine by God's grace.

BADUA: And your children?

BAABA: They are fine. They have gone to school.

BADUA: Are you still planning to send them to the boarding school?

BAABA: No Mama, that plan didn't work. Their father vehemently disagrees.

BADUA: Why?

BAABA: He says he can take care of them.

BADUA: Well! That should not be a problem. Let him manage the situation. Is everything set for your departure?

BAABA: Yes Mama.

BADUA: Great! Thank God. Remember everything I told you. Such opportunities come but once. Make the most out of everything. Be smart. Study hard but in all things, see this as a fresh start. I will be praying to St. Jude and the Blessed Lady for you.

BAABA: Thank you, Mama. I don't know what I would have done without you. You seem to be the only person who really empathises with me (*wiping tears*). Thank you very much.

BADUA: There is no need to cry. Whoever mounts a load on your neck does not mean harm. It is to strengthen your feeble neck. It is a lengthy race called life. Fill your sponge with water and believe that you can make it. The other time, I told you about what I have been through with your father. What I agreed to is not the best but sometimes the worst is the best. He won't die. What has to be done must be done. Water must surely find its level. If you sit at one place you sit on your own trouble. Go, go out there and find your destiny.

BAABA: Ok Mama. I won't give up. I have not only heard you. I understand you. My children need me and I will be there for them. How is Dada doing? You people nearly killed himooo (both laughing)

BADUA: He is there. The antibiotics seem to be working. The cough is not as bad as it used to though he didn't sleep all night. The doctor says this disease is difficult to cure but it can be cured. I am taking this year's novena seriously. I am hopeful that God will have mercy on him and heal him.

BAABA: Mama! (*laughing*) you weakened his immune system and now look at all these infections.

BADUA: What is it? (*laughing*) weakened what? He should thank God he still has something left in-between his legs.

BAABA: Mama, on a more serious note, I had a dream.

BADUA: Dream? What was it about?

BAABA: I dreamt about a dog chasing me.

BADUA: Dog! As in woof, woof? With a tail and teeth to bite? And did it bare its teeth at you?

BAABA: Yes Mama.

BADUA: Did it bite you?

BAABA: Somehow.

BADUA: How somehow? How do you mean by somehow? (*looking concerned*) The elders say, if the rain beats you say it beat you. Don't say it only splattered on you. Speak my daughter. Which of the two happened to you? Beat or splatter?

BAABA: Mama, I am serious. I didn't see it biting me but I tried hitting it with a stick and it run away.

BADUA: Aaah! (*laughing*) That is good to hear. That is good news, my dear. There is nothing to worry about.

BAABA: Except that when I woke up, I saw this on my leg (*bending to show her shin*)

BADUA: What is that?

BAABA: Teeth marks of the dog, I think.

BADUA: It is a lie. No way. The devil is a liar. There is nothing anybody can do to the child of my womb. I have suffered enough. Yes, I have (*unknotting her rapper and tightening it around her waist*). No child of mine will see the troubles I have seen in this world. I won't allow it. No way.

BAABA: (*looking frightened*) Mama, what is all this about? What does this mean? Talk to me. Am I going to die? What will happen to me? Can you explain? I am sure I am lost.

BADUA: It is nothing to be afraid of. It's a sign that evil eyes are watching us but don't worry your head over this. They will not succeed. Go to that university and lead a new life to the best of your ability. As for me your mother, I will remain here praying fervently for you. I will do what I have to do. Do you understand me? St. Jude will not let us down. Mother Mary will not let it happen. Go, go to the university.

BAABA: Yes Mama.

ACT 1

SCENE 3

*(Entering Kukua. Baaba and
Baadua already seated silently)*

KUKUA: Hello sister. Mama and I were talking
about you a few minutes ago.

BAABA: (*Faking cheerfulness*) Eiii! is that so?
She never mentioned it. Menopause,
I guess

KUKUA: Yes. It is true, ask Mama. They say
when you mention somebody's name
and the person doesn't show up then
it means the person is dead.

BADUA: (*laughing*) Dead paa. Anyway, that
is very true. Menopause is worrying
me but (*turning to Baaba*) you see
I told you we have been thinking
about you. I was just telling Kukua
that it will soon be her turn to go to

university. She will be visiting you often, when you go to school, to have an idea of life over there before next year.

BAABA: I can't wait. Mama, you have no idea how happy I am. *(Wiping a tear)*

KUKUA: Don't cry sister, life has its own way of solving our problems. It is good you are going away for some time. Everything will work out fine, you will see.

BAABA: Amen. Are we still prevented from seeing Dad?

BADUA: Laws are made to be broken. A single time will mean so much to him. It should not cause any problems. Here *(offering Baaba a nose mask)* cover your nose first. He will be so happy that you have come to see him. Let's go. *(all exiting)*

ACT 2

SCENE 1

(It's the second week of re-opening for the new academic year. Freshmen and women going about their registration. Baaba and Tessa share a single room with a balcony overlooking the famous Bojo Beach. The number 66 is inscribed on their door. Tessa is on her narrow single bed reading Ama Atta Aidoo's "Changes")

BAABA: *(talking to Tessa)* I'm visiting the campus this evening. Do you mind coming with me?

TESSA: That's ok, I don't mind. I don't seem to have much to do around here. But if I may ask, what exactly are we going to do? Remember the orientation titbits? "Always ask yourself what you are going to do there". The answer enables you to know the usefulness of the journey you are going to embark on.

BAABA: *(mockingly)* Eeeiiiii! Sharp brain. I hear you. I should be blessed to have you for a roommate. With your super memory, I don't have to make notes in class. MP3 recorder. You will record everything for me and then I will download when we come home.

(both laughing)

TESSA: You have nothing to worry about my dear. I am here. You can trust me. A friend tells me that regularity and punctuality coupled with reading ahead of the class and paying attention during lectures are the cardinal rules of academic success here. This is why I insist we go for lectures early and also sit in front. Ok, back to my question; where are we going to and what are we going to do there?

BAABA: Madam philosopher, please nothing much. We are just going to visit a friend I met a few days ago. Don't

ask me who, because you will know
when we get there?

TESSA: Yooo, I hear you. But how much time
are we supposed to spend there?

BAABA: *(laughing and dressing up)* Just
about ten minutes and nothing more.
Please, no more questions. Find out
the rest the answers to your question
when we get there. At least you know
I am not going to offer you for sale.
(both exiting and locking the door)

*(Osagyefo Hall, an all-male students' on-
campus residence. They knock on the door with
the inscription Students' Representative Council
(SRC) President. A male voice responds and
asks them to enter. Odum's room has a one and
half size bed on the right and a two in one futon
adjacent it. A 24-inch flat-screen television
hangs just above the tabletop fridge that stands
opposite that sofa. The sky-blue painting on the
walls illuminates the large image of Lord Byron
that occupies the wide space behind the sofa.
Baaba and Tessa knocking on Odum's door)*

ODUM: (*opening the door*) Hello, come in and make yourselves comfortable.

BAABA: *(Ignoring the armchair and sitting on the bed. Tessa perching on the tip of the armchair)* Thank you.

ODUM: May I ask what you care for, ladies?

TESSA: Any soft drink will do.

ODUM: Just a second, I will be back. *(stepping out and re-entering with three cans of Coca-Cola)* Sorry, this is not very cold.

BAABA: Oh! that is okay. Well, Odum, this is my friend and roommate Tessa. I should rather say my sister because we have known each other since primary school and destiny has brought us together here.

ODUM: *(shaking hands with Tessa)* Oh! I see. Nice meeting you. Are you also offering Classicalism?

TESSA: Yes. What of you?

ODUM: Same as you only that, I'm two years ahead. You will be surprised how this first year will quickly fly by. All the same, never mind, you'll soon get there, I mean the final year too. Have you started lectures?

BAABA: Mmm! not yet. When we do, we surely will be coming by for your assistance. Hope you won't mind?

ODUM: Sure, come on, I will be glad to be of any assistance to beautiful ladies like you. It's not much of a difficult programme. You only have to do your assignments, read constantly and just keep your cool. That's it. It's called academic issues. Please don't hesitate to knock on this door. That is, whenever you need any form of assistance, eh! (*smiling sheepishly*). It is always a pleasure to have beautiful ladies like you knocking on my door (stirring at Baaba and licking his lips). You can come and knock at any time and for any number of times. It will be opened to you (*still wearing the smile*).

BAABA: So, do you share this room with somebody?

ODUM: No. as the SRC president, I get to have this space to myself.

BAABA: Oooh! I see. And I guess you don't pay either.

ODUM: Surely, no.

BAABA: Eiii! I see. Then you are really enjoying.

ODUM: Are you sure about that? It is not as rosy as you think my dear. The position comes with very challenging tasks too. If you are able to get your grades right, I hope you will also consider taking up some positions. The benefits include having this small space to share with beautiful ladies like you. The experience is really worthwhile.

BAABA: Hahaha, (*laughing*) good you said someday. It really is a long way ahead but you never know, anything can happen. Whose image do you have here (*all turning to the image of Byron on the wall*)

ODUM: Lord Byron. (*Pointing to the picture*) That is my idol. Have you read any of his works?

TESSA: Yes, a couple of them when we were in the teacher training college.

ODUM: Oh! I see. Did you enjoy his works?

TESSA: Yes, his style but not his life.

ODUM: I know. You should be a feminist, I guess. Not many feminists like how he views and treats women. But it doesn't take much away from him. He is simply a beautiful writer who has the gift of interlocution. His ability to manipulate words in a way that mesmerizes the listener of his poems dazzles many scholars *(beginning to recite a Byron poem)*

She walks in beauty, like the night
Of cloudless climes and starry skies;
And all that's best of dark and bright
Meet in her aspect and her eyes:
Thus mellowed to that tender light
Which heaven to gaudy day denies.

One shade the more, one ray the less,
Had half impaired the nameless grace
Which waves in every raven tress,
Or softly lightens o'er her face;
Where thoughts serenely sweet express
How pure, how dear their dwelling place.

And on that cheek, and o'er that brow,
So soft, so calm, yet eloquent,
The smiles that win, the tints that glow,
But tell of days in goodness spent,
A mind at peace with all below,
A heart whose love is innocent!

TESSA: Wow! That was an impressive rendition of "She Walks In Beauty".

You recite it so well but you have to be careful you don't take after him. I hope his works inspire you and not his life. Have you ever read J.M. Coetzee's *Disgrace*?

ODUM: Ohhh! Yes, I see your point. I see where you are coming from and where you are heading towards.

TESSA: Good. Do you remember what happened to Lurie? I am sure he was obsessed with Byron and ended up behaving like him. So, when one says "Byron is my mentor", I don't hesitate to warn them.

ODUM: Yes Mum. You have a valid point there. But let me also say that you have just met me. When you get to know me, you will know how much respect I have for women. I am my mother's only male child. I have five sisters who took turns to take care of me when my dad died. My old boy died when I was only ten years old. So, you can imagine. I do not only respect women, but I also adore them and value them. It is my philosophy to worship them when they come my way because but for the love and care of the women in my life I would not be here.

TESSA: *(laughing)* I am serious though. It's ok to respect women. In fact, it is very important. But idolizing them can have a Lauric or Byronizing effect. Your mentor speaks pretty well about women but I fear this, especially in your case, may lead to your objectification of women. Often, we see men who claim they love their women so much that they would kill another man for lusting after their beautiful wives. I am just asking you to be careful. Love can easily birth hate.

ODUM: I hear you. For us Muslim converts, Allah forbids unjustified violence. The holy book encourages men to take care of women. You have nothing to fear about me.

BAABA: Haahaaaha (*laughing*), interesting one there from Miss Philosopher. You guys seem to have so much in common. Tessa here loves classical poetry. In fact, she is simply good at both crafting and reciting them. One of these days you should organize a poetry contest so that she can partake. Anyway, I guess it's getting late. We have to leave now. Thanks for the drink.

ODUM: Poetry makes you wise. You are blessed with wisdom for a friend. Anyway, you're welcome. (*seeing them off to his doorstep*) It is a delight being with you ladies. Hope to see you again soon. I won't be around throughout this week. The National Executive Committee is touring all public universities to see how well our fresh students are settling in.

BAABA: Alright. Then see you next two weeks perhaps.

ODUM: I have your number so I will call.
          Take care of yourselves then. Thank
          you for passing through.

BAABA: *(parting company with Odum)* We
          will again. Have a safe journey.

ODUM: *(speaking to himself)* Nice girl there.
          I think it's a deal. One down for the
          semester. Let's see what happens
          (smiling) But what was all that about?
          Her friend sounded suspicious. She is
          more mature. Such women are very
          difficult to handle. I just pray she
          wouldn't poison my girl. Next week,
          I will be back with full vigour. This
          one is taller than Akweley, and even
          prettier too. But Akwele too was
          goodooo. This one can be better.
          Baaba, that is such a romantic name.
          These tall women, hmmm, they will
          kill meooo.

ACT 2

SCENE 2

(It is late afternoon, Baaba entering the room and Tessa preparing supper)

TESSA: Baaba, Odum came by this afternoon just after you left for the campus.

BAABA: Oh! Yes. I met him.

TESSA: When?

BAABA: I passed by his place. He is a real gentleman and cooks very well.

TESSA: Did he cook for you?

BAABA: Not really, he invited me and I couldn't reject it. That's all. Nothing much.

TESSA: Invited you to cook or to come and be cooked for?

BAABA: (*laughing*) Tess you are funny.

TESSA: Me rather? Baaba, be carefulooooooo.
         I felt something unusual the last time
         we visited and now it looks like your
         visits are becoming frequent. You are
         a married mother.

BAABA: Come on Tessa. You remind me
         of my Auntie. Whenever she calls,
         she would say Kobina says this and
         that and then she will end it all by
         saying "Baaba be carefulooo" This
         is ordinary campus life. Besides I'm
         careful. Stop worrying about me ok!
         Big Sister.

TESSA: No, school mother *(both laughing)*
         I am only cautioning you because I
         hear guys here can be very cunning,
         including some lecturers too. They
         can pretend to be interested in helping
         you with your studies only to take
         advantage of you. Your engagement
         ring too, can be very deceptive. It's
         more like a fashion ring and therefore
         easy to ignore. Remember also that
         your husband has not hidden his

displeasure about you coming to school. He thinks I convinced you to come to school. I am not even sure what his fears are but he has made us clear about his dislike for your coming to school agenda. If anything happens to you, you know I will take all the blame. I don't want any trouble, my dear. Yoooo!

BAABA: I get your point. It's cool with me. Kobina even called when I was with Odum. Surprisingly, he asked me where I was and what I was doing. Hmm! Men can be very sensitive.

TESSA: The two shall be one, remember? It's just a warning shot. I hear many marriages break up here on campus. Don't entertain anything like that happening to you. You have your girls. Let's concentrate on our books and leave here in peace, not in pieces.

BAABA: I believe those that broke up marriages already had their fissures before either couple came to school. I agree that coming to school can sometimes exacerbate tension in a marriage. Come to think of it, a suffering partner deserves a break. In addition, any good marriage should stand the test of time. As for a bad marriage, school is a good means of getting rid of it.

TESSA: But I think that sometimes hearing the stories told about other people's marriages is a therapy for saving one's own weak marriage. Unless the school is used as a ploy to end that marriage someway, somehow (*stirring suspiciously at Baaba*).

BAABA: Anyway, Odum asked me to come for some books so I'll be back.

TESSA: (*untrustworthily*) Can't it wait till tomorrow? It's late.

BAABA: No, he's travelling tomorrow. Are you coming with me?

TESSA: Nope! I think I need some sleep when
              I am done with this *banku.*

*(Exit Baaba. Tessa pulls her sleeping
cloth over her head to sleep)*

ACT 2

SCENE 3

(A few weeks into the semester, ODUM knocks and enters. Baaba is in a crumpled T-shirt only. Odum draws her to himself, his hands under her T-shirt, up unto her breast and gives both nipples gentle squeeze. She nags with the slightest resistance)

BAABA: No Odum! This is bad timing. Tessa has not gone far she will soon return.

ODUM: *(zipping up and giving her a hand off the floor)* I'm sorry; I was carried away by your sexy look. *(Gives her a deep kiss).*

BAABA: That was very risky. The other time we were nearly caught. Today would have been terrible.

ODUM: Sorry honey! *(arms wrapping around her waist)* It won't happen like this again. I promise. That is why I prefer you coming to visit me rather than me coming over. I am in that room alone so we have all the privacy in the world. Here, we are always cautious about one thing or the other. On the other hand, you can let me rent a room for you somewhere. Then when I come over, we won't have to worry about this or that. I can even come and spend the night without any interruptions.

BAABA: I told you to give me time to think about that.

ODUM: Anyway, *(letting go of her)* I just passed by to see how you were doing. Will you come over tonight? We'll have fun in privacy. Ok! *(Moving a bit close to her and kissing her forehead. She does not resist)*

BAABA: Alright, I will, but you have to take lunch before you leave. P-l-e-e-a-a-s-e.

ODUM: Ok. *(eating the meal quickly and kisses her goodbye. Tessa entering just as he turns to leave)* Hello Tessa, just passed by to say hello. In fact, I was on my way out. So, see you later.

TESSA: *(slightly stunned)* Ok bye. *(To Baaba)* What is going on here? You entertain a male visitor dressed like this and feed him?

BAABA: Ok, I guess this is the time to spill it. The truth is that Odum and I are in a relationship.

TESSA: *(eye narrowing in shock)* What! Are you crazy? You are married with kids. For Christ sake, do you care?

BAABA: *(calmly)* Come on, don't scream so much about this, Ok! It's nothing serious just like good friends nothing more. I just want to experience how having a relationship outside marriage feels like that's all. Besides, this is a university and everybody is mature. I appreciate your concern, but believe me I know what I'm doing.

TESSA: *(shaking head in disbelief and sighing)* Hmmm.

(Baaba's cell phone ringing)

BAABA: Hello!

KOBINA ESAN: Sweetheart, how are you doing? And with your books?

BAABA: Very fine. How about you and the kids? You don't sound very cheerful.

KOBINA ESAN: Yeah, we're fine only that we miss mummy. Besides, business is not very encouraging. I sold only one fender today. But I'm sure tomorrow will be better. I have placed the order for your car. It should be ready soon.

BAABA: Ok dear, thank you. I will continue to pray for you. Please don't worry too much. Take good care of yourself as well as the little ones. Ok!

KOBINA ESAN: Alright Baby, I will. You also have to take care of that beautiful body for us. Don't allow those young riff ruffs to touch it. Ok! I will always love you and be there for you.

BAABA: Ok. My love bye.

KOBINA ESAN: Bye my heart. Extend my greetings to Tessa.

BAABA: Bye. *(Hanging up and smiling)*

TESSA: *(Whispering as she dishes her meal)* Hmm what a pity!

BAABA: Hey! Hey! Stop feeling like that girl. Please don't tell anybody about Odum and me.

TESSA: Me! Forget it. I don't have that time. Just tell those friends of yours not to think of coming to interrogate me again else, they'll have the shock of their lives.

BAABA: Did Barbara ask you anything? Don't mind her, didn't she do worse things than this? Even after she met her husband, she had male and female affairs. Who is she to advise somebody? If I were in her shoes, I would be thinking of how to make a baby after all the operations and womb flashing. I know she only pretends to like me. She is, in fact, envious of me.

TESSA: Really! Pretends? Envious? I s-e-e-e-e.

BAABA: Oh yes! What do you think? I know her inside out. Look, her struggle with not being able to get pregnant is as a result of the many abortions she carried out with her husband before they got married. That is why he is willing to spend all the money in the world on her. If you think she is a saint, my sister, forget it. She's nobody.

TESSA: Eeeiii! *(opening mouth ajar)*

BAABA: Yes, now she's gone home for an operation. Something concerning ovarian cyst and something. She's nosy about my affairs because of envy.

TESSA: Don't talk like that about her. She is your friend. Besides, she's not here and it's not fair. You like her that is why you even spend the night with her right?

(Barbara, shouting Baaba's name from outside, in the corridor that leads up to Baaba's room. opening the door without knocking, she steps in, closing the door behind her)

BARBARA: Hello ladies, good afternoon and how are you doing?

BOTH: Very fine.

BARBARA: Thank God. I heard your voices from the stairway. *(Baaba and Tessa steal a surprise glance at each other without comment)* I'm on my way home as I informed you earlier. I will be back on Monday. Please submit my assignment for me *ai. (Handing a sheet of paper to Baaba)*

BAABA: Oh ok! *(Taking the paper)* Let's go then. I will see you off *(To Tessa)* Are you ready, T?

(Turning to Barbara) We were on our way to the library *(putting on a pair of jeans, grabs her bag and all three exit)*

ACT 2

SCENE 4

(It's the beginning of the first semester of the second academic year. Baaba gains residential accommodation and moves to campus whiles Tessa remains off-campus. Fiifi and Baako are friends and roommates. They lay idle on their beds on a hot afternoon)

FIIFI: Charlie what is this I hear in town?

BAAKO: About what?

FIIFI: About you, Baaba, and Odum.

BAAKO: *(laughing to scorn)* That nice girl? I'm not aware she's for him, besides, to me she's just one of the many. Nothing serious and nothing much.

FIIFI: How serious?

BAAKO: It's just last semester and with this latest information, believe me when I say it's over. She's expired.

FIIFI: You think Odum is aware of the two of you?

BAAKO: None of my business.

FIIFI: And are you aware she's married with kids?

BAAKO: Come off it boy, did she tell you that herself?

FIIFI: It's true my brother.

BAAKO: My good Jesus! Women are satanic.

FIIFI: Wow! Hold it. Are you giving me the impression that you don't know about this too?

(There's a knock on the door. Fiifi goes to see who is there)

FIIFI: Hey Baaba! *(turning to Baako)* It's Baaba.

41

BAAKO: Heiii! Baaba, come in.

FIIFI: *(picking up some books and heading toward the door)* I'm off to the library see you later, Baaba.

BAABA: Alright.

(*Exit Fiifi*)

BAAKO: You are looking gorgeous. Are you ready for the beach?

BAABA: Yeah! I'm more than ready.

BAAKO: Eeeiish! I like the spirit. It will be an exciting time with you. *(holding her hand, he gives her a kiss on the forehead, dresses up, checks the content of his wallet and leaves with her)*

ACT 2

SCENE 5

(A week later. Longman hall room 90, Tessa is in Baaba's room for a visit. Baaba goes to the washroom which is a couple of doors away. Baako knocks and enters)

BAAKO: Hi!

TESSA: Hi. What brings you here?

BAAKO: I just passed by to say hello.

TESSA: To whom? Look at you. Sit.

BAAKO: *(sitting on Baaba's bed)* Thanks, I'm glad to meet you today. There's something I want to ask you.

TESSA: *(indifferently)* Spit it. I'm all ears.

BAAKO: Is your friend married with kids?

TESSA: Why do you ask me and not her? Can't you see the ring on her finger?

BAAKO: Isn't it for fun? You know these ladies and their fashion sense. Isn't it one of such things?

TESSA: *(sternly)* Look here, Baako or whatever you call yourself, Baaba is married with kids and the ring she wears is not for fun. If she told you it is, then it's a big lie.

BAAKO: *(Bowing head for a moment in despair)* Tessa, believe me, I was not aware.

TESSA: *(Snapping)* And how did you become aware?

BAAKO: From my roommate when he told me about the rumours concerning her and Odum.

TESSA: *(shaking head remorsefully)* Hmmm!

BAAKO: *(After a period of silence)* I'm very sorry. I now understand why you hate me so much. Please forgive me and trust me when I say it's over between us. Please.

TESSA: If you say so. But I know God will deal with all of you one after the other. All you know is to jump from one lady to the other. You guys just cannot stay with one lady.

BAAKO: But …

TESSA: *(cutting in)*But what?

BAAKO: She is your friend; how come you are not like that? Do you advise her?

TESSA: Look here, Mr Devil turned BORN AGAIN, we've been friends for over ten years. If you care to know, it is not for somebody like you to tell us how to walk and talk. Do I make myself clear?

BAAKO: Anyway, you have a point. I'm sorry. I have to you leave now thanks for the reception.

TESSA: *(indifferently)* You're welcome.

(Baaba entering soon after Baako's exit)

45

TESSA: What's that envelope in your hand?

BAABA: Yeah. I picked it from the porter's lodge downstairs. It's a letter from Nana, my cousin in the UK.

TESSA: Really! What does he say?

BAABA: *(Opening it with a smile)* Nothing much, it's just the document I need to process my papers.

TESSA: *(Looking slightly confused)* Which papers?

BAABA: I intend to travel abroad this vacation. Please don't tell anybody about this. Not even Kobby is aware.

TESSA: *(Wearing a little smile on her face)* Kobina Esan, your husband, is not aware?

BAABA: Yes, he will not allow it if he gets to know.

TESSA: And where are you getting the money from?

BAABA: Well, Barbara introduced me to a friend who is willing to help at no cost. He's a very generous guy.

TESSA: *(Still smiling, hands akimbo and shaking her head)* Baaba, why are you doing this to yourself?

BAABA: Doing what? Ehhh! You see I always tell you that had it not been for the pregnancy that came in, there was no way I would have married Kobina Esan. That bastard informed my parents before I knew it and ignorantly, they also forced me to marry him. Ha! I loved Jeffrey and we had plans to get married. As I speak, honestly, I love Odum dearly. So much so that if I had the chance, I would flee with him to anywhere outside the country and get married to him. *(spitefully)* Kobina Esan, Kyia-a-a-a.

TESSA: *(looking surprised with disgust)* Are you normal? Look at you. Are you not ashamed of yourself and what you are doing? Of what use is this Odum to you? Is he the one helping you to make the 'A's? I guess not. And you have the nerves to look at me in the eye and talk like that. *(Shaking the head in disbelief)* Anyway, I have to leave now. The group members should be waiting. I don't like to be late for group assignments.

BAABA: *(clearing her throat)* Is our Farrouk visiting?

TESSA: Nooo, I told you that the man is too old for me. Besides he is a Hindu.

BAABA: So? *(astonishingly)* He is sweet, gentle and generous. What else can a woman want in a man? Whoa!

TESSA: I knowww. But my church won't allow it. He is an unbeliever.

BAABA: Do you love him?

TESSA: Who wouldn't?

BAABA: Then be fastooo. There are hunters all over my sister. Make up your mind before you regret the delay. Let's get going. You will be late. I want to see my big sister off.

(Seeing Tessa off, Baaba's cell phone rings)

TESSA: Are you not coming for the discussion? I will join you in an hour. I need some sleep.

BAABA: *(signalling ok to Tessa she responds to the call)* Hello! *(Beginning to walk towards Barbara's room, a block away)*

KOBINA ESAN: *(lying on his bed)* Good evening dear. How are you, sweetheart?

BAABA: *(flatly)* Very fine. Why didn't you call me as you promised?

KOBINA ESAN: Sorry, I went to clear some items from the harbour.

BAABA: Is my car ready?

KOBINA ESAN: Yes, but I couldn't pick it up because the money I had was not enough. I intend getting some more money to do the final payment. So, no need to worry right?

BAABA: Oh sweetie! I have all the patience in this world only that life is a little tough without a ride on campus.

KOBINA ESAN: When are you coming home to see us?

BAABA: Maybe this weekend.

KOBINA ESAN: I miss you.

BAABA: I know that. Don't worry I will come home soon. Take care.

KOBINA ESAN: Well then goodnight. Remember to extend my greetings to T. *(speaking to himself)* Why is she so cold? Is it the car? Or she knows... What could she know? No! But, and, but, or... No! there is fire on the mounting. What can I do? The father again? Noooo, the old man should be angry with me. The mother? Naaa, that woman doesn't want to even see my face. Then who? T? Tessa, No! I suspect I have lost her too. *(pacing about)*. I need to do something but what?

(Baaba entering Barbara's room)

BARBARA: I thought you wouldn't show up. Did you tell Tessa where you were going to?

BAABA: Nope!

BARBARA: That girl is something so don't be telling her things about us.

(singing, praying and preaching from a radio sitting on the window sill in Tessa's room. Singing stops and a voice on the radio begins a sermon. Entering Baaba)

TESSA: Hello Baaba, come in. How are you?

BAABA: Very well and you?

TESSA: I am good. You look worn out. Why didn't you show up for the discussions last night?

BAABA: Oh! you know I told you I will. It's only that my stomach was aching that is why I didn't show up. I had everything right to come.

(Clear audible voice of voice preaching on the radio:

> *Repent, my brothers and sisters, for the kingdom of God is at hand. Keep your path straight so that you may find favour with the Lord. Seek the face of the Lord. Stop your sinful ways. Be faithful to God in all you do. Faithfulness is a requirement for God's grace. Learn to be sincere. Fidelity is righteousness. What do you want in this world? The Bible says we do not belong to this world. We are only passing through. The day of the Lord is near. If you hear*

my voice this morning, harden not
your heart. Harken to me. Return to
your God. He is merciful...

TESSA: Ameen! So, does it feel better this morning?

BAABA: What?

TESSA: Your stomach, of cause?

BAABA: Is that thing not too loud?

TESSA: *(interjecting)* No, it is not.

What are you looking for my sister? What are
you looking for, brother?
Return to the Lord. He is the only one who
can give you happiness and
satisfaction. Man cannot make man happy.
Woman cannot make woman
happy. Look up to God for happiness and
satisfaction. The flesh will let you
down. The world will disappoint you...

TESSA: You were with Barbara, right?

BAABA: (laughs)Yeah, but I left earlier till I fell sick in my tummy.

TESSA: Baaba, I don't care about what goes on between you and that friend of yours. We are not children and everybody knows what is good for her. But remember that you sit next to me. I can't refuse to teach you when you ask me. I only believe that if we put in a little more effort in our studies, we could make better grades. Also, remember that Barbara sits beside Emma and she gets help from her. We came here for our grades and that must remain our priority. I am taking my referred paper tomorrow. I suggest you go for the discussion so you can brief me after my paper. What do you think?

BAABA: *(Sarcastically)* It's ok with me. It's only strange how you were referred. We sit next to each other. We wrote almost the same thing. You even taught me throughout the exam. So how come I made a B and you failed the paper? Very strange but I wish you all the best in tomorrow's *Second World War.*

TESSA: Sounds more like a teaser but trust me I will make an 'A' to prove a point.

BAABA: I trust you and I believe you can do it. You have to do it to mute those gossips.

ACT 3

SCENE 1

(Semester IV begins. Tuesday morning. Prof. Quist introduces himself to the class. All applaud to welcome him. Lectures begin with him and it is Modern English Classics)

QUIST: Good morning class. *(they respond)* My name is PROFESSOR NICHODEMOUS QUIST.

(Class mummering) You will be seeing me often. I will be taking you through Modern English Classics. So, relax, get your minds ready as we hit the ground running. *(class bursting into laughter)*

Ok, Keep quiet. *(Turning to write on the board)* We often Literature is a fictional replica of life. That is why it makes sense to all its readers across the globe. Shakespeare's plays and

56

poems are examples of Literature with global appeal. In the realms of the novel, nothing much can be said without mentioning Daniel Defoe's novels…

BAABA: *(To Tessa)* We are in for a real course this semester. I hate reading these old English novels. *(To herself)* There should be a way out.

TESSA: Ei! Baaba, the way this lecturer talks scares me. His lecture style calls for rapt attention and concentration. This time we have to come to class a little bit earlier so that we can sit in front of everyone else.

BAABA: Yes, that is true. But can't anybody tell him to open his mouth a little wider? What is that?

TESSA: *(laughing and speaking in a very low voice)* Maybe you should tell him. Don't you know he is from America?

BAABA: Is that why he talks through his nose and under his teeth? Eiii! Asemoo.

A STUDENT: *(raising hand up)* Ehh sir, it looks as if we are in for a course this semester. Some of us would like to know where you live so that we can come over for assistance in case we don't understand something.

CLASS: Yes, that is important.

QUIST: However, if I say something and you don't understand, just prompt me. Some of the other classes I teach have already said I speak too fast.

CLASS: *(in unison)* Yes! Yes! That is very true! We can't hear anything. *(One student shouts)* only "wrish" "wrish" "wrish" "wrish".

QUIST: You have your course outline. Read ahead for easy and enjoyable classes. Thank you.

BAABA: *(indifferently)* Hmmm.

QUIST: Does anyone know my house? Well, I think a few of you should know there. Anybody? *(Nobody responds)* Oh, what a shame! Anyway, it's Bungalow no 19, Lecturers' Flat. It's not very difficult to find. Simply described, it is right behind the Nkrumah Statue. On the other hand, I brought some books from Brendel University in New York. You may also pass by for some copies. They may be of great help to you.

QUIST: Can we borrow them?

QUIST: If only you will return them. I also brought some more books for the departmental library so you can access those. On that note, we end our class for today. Your course representative will communicate your first reading assignment to you by close of day. Have a good day.

STUDENTS: Thank you sir *(all rising to exit)*

(Later in the afternoon, Tessa and Baaba look for Mr QUIST's office and pay him a visit. They knock on the door and they are allowed entry)

TESSA and BAABA: *(together)* Good afternoon Sir.

QUIST: Hi, guess I met you in my class, right?

BOTH: *(pleasantly)* Yes Sir.

QUIST: So, have you closed for the day?

TESSA: Yes Sir.

QUIST: Do you come from this town?

TESSA: Here? No sir. We are both from Elmina

QUIST: Sorry, I didn't even ask your names.

TESSA: I'm Theresa Sarah Sackey and my friend is Baaba Mentel Sackey.

QUIST: Hey! Are you siblings, cousins or something?

TESSA: Not really, just friends. We just happen to have the same surnames.

QUIST: And you are friends.

TESSA: Yes sir.

QUIST: That's good. So, are you enjoying my lectures?

TESSA: Yes, but I fear it will be difficult as we move forward. Classics is not my favourite. English Literature is quite complex. That's what makes it difficult.

BAABA: With the projector, does it mean we can't have reading handouts or notes?

QUIST: Hmm! Probably not. Is that a problem?

TESSA: Certainly!

QUIST: Then I'll find a way out. How about printing out my slides for you? Will that help?

TESSA: Yes, it will greatly, I believe.

QUIST: What else is a problem with my class?

*(hesitatingly, they take a quick
glance at each other)*

BAABA: Sir, Tessa says the way you talk.

QUIST: *(breaks into laughter)* And what do you say pretty face?

BAABA: *(smiles coyly)* I think you talk too fast and too undertone.

QUIST: You think and not Tessa?

BAABA: Both of us, I mean.

QUIST: How would you prefer that I talk my dear?

BAABA: Maybe you should just slow your speech a bit and open your mouth a little bit more.

QUIST: I see. I had a similar request from the other classes I teach. However, as I already said in class, please draw my attention when I run too fast or speak too low. Maybe I should let you be my monitors. So periodically I will look at your faces for your reaction.

TESSA: That is fine.

BOTH: Ok thank you, Sir.

BAABA: Please we will like to take our leave.

QUIST: Alright. Thank you for passing by.

ACT 3

SCENE 2

(Baaba's room on campus. Odum entering meets Tessa)

ODUM: Hello Tessa. Good evening.

TESSA: Good evening. She's gone out.

ODUM: *(smiling)* That was snappy. Out where?

TESSA: Sorry I just came in so I don't really know. You have her number so why don't you call her and find out?

ODUM: I tried but her phone is out of coverage area.

TESSA: Well keep trying if you REALLY can't live without her.

ODUM: You don't really like me. Do you? What have I done wrong? Is it wrong to love your friend?

TESSA: Not when you know she's married with kids.

ODUM: Has Baako been coming here?

TESSA: Sorry, I hardly come by these days so I don't know.

ODUM: Alright, I am leaving please when she returns tell her I was here.

TESSA: Who?

ODUM: Baaba of course!

TESSA: Oh! Okay.

(Odum leaves and Baaba enters a couple of minutes later)

TESSA: Did you get the book?

BAABA: Yes. Finally, I got it from Aya. Sally is not in. I learnt from her roommate that she has travelled out of town. Luckily, on my way back I met Aya and when I asked her, she willingly offered me her copy.

TESSA: Thank God. When are you supposed to return it?

BAABA: She didn't say.

TESSA: Great. Then we have to make a copy quickly.

BAABA: We'll send it when we finish with the assignment.

TESSA: (speaking *with a flat tone*) Odum just left. Did you meet him on your way in?

BAABA: No. What did he want?

TESSA: *(sounding surprised)* What did you just say?

BAABA: I thought he left a message.

TESSA: Not really, He only wants you to know he passed by. He also wanted to know what was up with you and Baako.

BAABA: Why would he ask? I wonder who has been feeding him with all those kinds of stuff.

TESSA: He was wondering where you have been all afternoon.

BAABA: *(Laughing out loud)* Hahahaaa. *(To Tessa)* I will see him tomorrow. *(To herself)* So Odum now knows about Baako and me. But Baako is history? Interesting! I already have the residence and he can't take it from me. What do I tell him tonight? I'll make love to him then he will be reassured and trust me. I need to work fast on QUIST. That girl STUDENT 2, what was she doing in QUIST's house this afternoon? Ei! She's such a smart girl. This QUIST guy is slow but sure. I'm sure STUDENT 2 gave him a germ bite. But she wasn't jealous of my presence. Who cares? Will she tell Odum? Not sure. No, she won't. If she does, what will I do? Or she already has? Let them all please themselves, in fact, let them go to hell.

ACT 3

SCENE 3

(In Odum's residence, off-campus. Baaba knocks and enters. ODUM in boxer shorts only draws Baaba close to him. They start kissing. Odum gradually drags her to his bed. His tongue rolls up her belly as his fingers crawl up to her already hardened nipples. Baaba moans slightly with pleasure. Odum pushes all the clothes and books on the bed with his left leg, making more room for them on the bed. He puts his tongue in her ear as she continues to moan pleasurably. In a soft whisper, he tells her how he missed her. He rubs his hardness on her lower abdomen as he lay flat on her. Gently, whiles still sucking her ear, Odum lifts up her skirt and thrusts himself into her. They lay beside each other, both exhausted and starring into the ceiling.)

ODUM: *(Seemingly angry)* I was expecting to see you yesterday. Did your roommate tell you I passed by?

BAABA: Yes, I was busy with my assignment. I could not finish on time. Did you miss me?

ODUM: Yes, and I was worried because I couldn't reach you too. Anyway, now you are here and we are together everything else can wait. Will you spend the night with me?

BAABA: Oh! Odum dear, I have assignments to finish. Please let me go.

ODUM: Go where? Bring it up. I'll do them for you. Besides, I told you not to worry. Since when did assignments determine your grade? Which course is that and who teaches you?

BAABA: English Classicalism by Prof QUIST.

ODUM: No problem, I worked out your residence. I can handle this one too. Trust me!

BAABA: I didn't like your approach to the other course. Tessa is my friend.

Couldn't you have chosen another person? Now she has to re-sit the paper and any time she mentions it, I feel guilty.

ODUM: Sorry about that. Next time you will choose whose grades get swapped.

BAABA: Maybe you should teach me how you do the swapping. What do you think?

ODUM: It's a complex process but I will, though not now.

(He strips her nude, they make love again with passion and they fall asleep locked in arms. Lights go off. Baaba wakes up next morning, dresses up and heads towards Tessa's residence whilst Odum still sleeps)

BAABA: Good morning.

TESSA: Good morning. How are you?

BAABA: Fine and you?

TESSA: Cool. I was at your end this morning. Your roommate told me you did not spend the night there.

BAABA: Yes, I was with Barbara.

TESSA: Sure? She asked me about you this morning.

BAABA: Fine, the truth is I spent the night with Odum.

TESSA: What! You did what? And what if Kobby gets to know?

BAABA: Never mind he'll never know unless you tell him. Besides, who cares? The issue here is love, not marriage. Aside from that, Odum helps me with school work and others. Do you know what your Kobby is doing at home? Kobina Esan has his own moves at home.

TESSA: What is he doing? Rumours. That is all you have. No evidence.

BAABA: *(smiling)* That is even the least of my problems *wai*, my sister.

(knocking on the door. Baaba responds. Kobina Esan enters. Both slightly shocked)

KOBINA ESAN: Hello good morning ladies.

BOTH: Good morning.

BAABA: *(looking astonishingly at Kobina)* Wow! You didn't tell me you were coming over.

TESSA: *(Before Esan could answer)* Come on in and take a seat. *(He sits)* Welcome. What calls for this unexpected visit? We just returned from lectures.

KOBINA ESAN: Thank you "T". How are you doing?

TESSA: We are very good. School life is never easyooo but we are trying.

KOBINA ESAN: Well, I came to transact business in town so I decided to pass by and just say hello. In that case,

I'm on my way. I brought you, ladies, some items they are in the car.

BAABA: How are the kids doing?

KOBINA ESAN: Everything and everybody is fine.

BAABA: *(Turning to Tessa)* I'll see Kobby off.

TESSA: Oh! so soon, ok. Safe journey then *(Esan and Tessa hug briefly)*

(Exiting Baaba and Kobina Esan. Baaba returns shortly with food items)

TESSA: You have such a lovely husband but you still do what you like, as though you were not married. Some want but no get, you get but no want. *(she sighs)* Hmmm. That's the irony of life.

BAABA: *(Entering with some yams)* Remember to take some of these away.

TESSA: Baaba, the signals are getting closer and stronger. Are you sure you know the consequences of what you are doing and you are ready for it?

BAABA: And who says I'm worried about this man. Maybe he is worried about me.

TESSA: You have to end this lifestyle somehow somewhere. It doesn't speak well of a pretty young woman like you.

BAABA: Come on Tessa, this is not the time to talk about this. Let's go we'll be late for the Quist *(both exiting)*

ACT 3

SCENE 4

(In class, a colleague walking up to Baaba)

STUDENT 2: Hi princess, you're looking sweet this morning.

BAABA: Thanks.

STUDENT 2: Jay asked me to tell you to see him.

BAABA: When?

STUDENT 2: Didn't say.

BAABA: When did he tell you this?

STUDENT 2: This morning. On my way here.

BAABA: Alright thank you

(Entering PROFESSOR QUIST)

QUIST: Good morning class. Today we will continue with the issue of "The History of English Literary Classicalism". The novel as a genre started out as a journal record and then short story publications and memoirs. Daniel Defoe is credited with the title, the father of the English novel for his classical piece titled, *Robinson Crusoe*. He also has to his credit another classical titled, *Moll Flanders*. Sir Walter Scott's *Quintin Durward* is another classical work… For your project on this topic write up a list of classic English novels, their authors and their year of publication. I will collect them at the next lecture. *(QUIST and Baaba exchanging glances as class disperses)*

(Baaba entering Jay's, the academic counsellor's office)

JAY: Hi, come in and take a seat. Sorry to bother you this morning. How are you?

BAABA: *(Taking a seat on the opposite end of the table behind which Jay sits).* Very fine Sir. I got your message from my colleague. This is why I am here.

JAY: Good! I am sure you are wondering why I called you right?

BAABA: *(Nodding in approval)*

JAY: Well, I just want to tell you that first of all you are a very beautiful young woman whom every man would want. In fact, you are what a man calls magically sweet and seductive.

BAABA: *(Baaba smiling and looking away shyly)*

JAY: It's true. You are very lovely and very exceptional. Come to think of the fact that you are a mother is even more amazing. But my major concern is on your relationships on campus. As your counsellor, I haven't called you here to ask you how true that is. I only want to tell you that if it is true that you are flirting with or dating that multiple people, please quit immediately. This does not suit a respectable married mother like you. Your kind of beauty will match better with decency and self-discipline and this is what I want to see in you. Right? You are intelligent. Study hard and make your own grades. Your current situation can have psychological effects on you and your family. I don't want to talk about your husband. However, you know what you have to do...

BAABA: Alright Sir.

JAY: Are you through with lectures for the day?

BAABA: No sir, one more to go.

JAY: Then I will leave you to go and prepare for that. Thank you for coming

BAABA: Thank you Sir *(Exiting Baaba)*

(Tessa reading on a bed in Baaba's room on Campus. Entering Baaba)

TESSA: Hi, you are back. Did you meet Jay?

BAABA: *(sounding sad)* Yes, good afternoon. Somebody told him about Odum and me. I think he's right about all he said. I have decided to end it with him.

TESSA: *(Looking surprised)* Somebody? This university talks. Well, it is good you find wisdom in whatever it is he said.

(Entering Naana, a course mate)

NAANA: Hello Tessa, Baaba are you asleep? It's Friday night what plans do you, ladies, have?

TESSA: Nothing yet.

NAANA: Really! Then that's good. Hmm, can you ladies, please, see me off to a place this evening?

TESSA: *(Stirring Naana from the corners of her eyes)*

79

BAABA: Which place?

NAANA: Come with me and I will show you.

(Turning to Tessa) Miss, please are you not coming?

TESSA: No, madam. As you can see, I want to finish reading this book by close of day.

BAABA: *(To Naana)* Ok, just a minute

(Dressing up. Turning to Tessa) I will be back soon.

NAANA: *(Both exiting)* You know, Honourable Amponsah proposed to me earlier and I refused. Now he has promised me a sponsorship package. He asked me to come for it today. I need the money for my SRC election campaign but I don't want to go there alone so please accompany me *wai*. Pl-e-e-e-a-s-e, I beg you.

BAABA: Ok. So, what time do you have in mind?

NAANA: 7 pm should be fine.

BAABA: Ok.

NAANA: Thank you. I will come by at 7:00 pm then.

BAABA: Ok. But first, remember that we are not spending the whole evening there.

NAANA: Promise.

BAABA: *(Returning to the room. Tessa giving her a quizzical look)* Haahaahhha! So now what is with the look?

TESSA: Go ahead, what is the new deal, who is the new catch?

BAABA: Ahhhh! I thought as much. Anyway, she wants me to see her off to Hon. Amponsah's house for a sponsorship package.

TESSA: Is this friend of yours serious about the presidency?

BAABA: Oh yes, she is preparing very hard. She is serious.

TESSA: *(Heading for the door).*All the best to her then. I have some things to do so we will meet, God willing, tomorrow

BAABA: *(Walking her out)* Alright.

(Naana and Baaba pressing the bell on gate number 44, Fox Street. A servant opens)

SERVANT: Good evening. Please come in, Madams.

NAANA: How are you Boko?

SERVANT: Very fine Madam.

NAANA: Is your master in?

BOKO: Yes. He is expecting you. Please come in.

NAANA: Thank you.

(opening the door to the main house. Enter Naana with Baaba following her. Hon. Amponsah rises with an exclamation, hugs them one after another beginning with Naana)

HON. AMPONSAH: Good to see you, beautiful ladies. Please make yourselves comfortable.

(Calling out the servant) Boko, Boko, Boko.

SERVANT: Yes Master.

HON. AMPONSAH: *(Boko appearing)* Come in here. Please bring my ladies some water and some drinks.

(Boko leaving and returning with a tray of water and cans of soft drinks)

You have such a beautiful friend here. I am Honourable Amponsah

(extending a hand to Baaba who returns the exchange)

BAABA: *And I am Baaba.*

NAANA: *(Turning to Honourable Amponsah)* Okay, enough pleasantries. Baaba is my coursemate and a very good friend.

(Turning to Baaba) Baaba, this is Honourable Amponsah. I have already said so much about him. He is very sweet and generous. But for him, I would not know how to carry out my campaign.

HON. AMPONSAH: Oh please! You are flattering me. *(To Baaba)* Don't mind all the things Naana is saying. She is really good at making my head swell.

NAANA: Hahahaaaa. You see, you have a way of making me look bad before my cronies. You don't know what everything you do for me means to me. *(turning to Baaba)* Sorry about that. We nearly forgot you were here. *(reaching out to Hon. Amponsah's his hands)* We have to go now. I just wanted to say thank you.

HONOURABLE AMPONSAH: *(Kissing her on the lips)* So soon? I thought we could go out for supper.

NAANA: Noooo, another time, maybe. We have assignments and group discussions to take care of. We have to leave now. *(Honourable Amponsah seeing them off)*

ACT 3

SCENE 5

(In Tessa's Room. Baaba ending a conversation on the phone)

TESSA: *(Talking to Baaba)* So how did you get to know Hon. Amponsah?

BAABA: Through Naana of cause? Don't you remember when she asked me to accompany her to his house for some package?

TESSA: Your friend Naana?

BAABA: Yes Mum.

TESSA: And is there anything else about him that you think I should know?

BAABA: Him, who?

TESSA: The Mr. Honourable.

BAABA: Eeeei! Eeei! I knew you would ask me this question. Fine, Honourable Amponsah said he liked me.

TESSA: Hahahahahaaaaa. My girl, you are possessed. Whoa!

BAABA: *(indifferently)*By what? He likes me! For friendship nothing more.

TESSA: Just that? And you've since been visiting so that even the servants seem to know you so well? Is he not married?

BAABA: How do you know that?

TESSA: Am I deaf? Didn't I just hear the conversation you two had on the phone?

BAABA: His wife is not in town. Besides, they are on the verge of divorce. I made it clear to him that a second wife is out of the question.

TESSA: So why do you go visiting him? And is he not seeing your friend Naana?

BAABA: W-e-e-e-ll, I don't know about Naana and him. Moreover, I told you we are friends and I like him that is why I visit him. I help him solve some of his problems in his constituency. I think I like his company too. *(Picks a book from Tessa's bed)* Is this your book?

TESSA: No, I picked it from your room yesterday. Where did you get it from and why haven't you told me about it?

BAABA: *(smiles)* You know I don't hide anything from you. Prof. QUIST gave this and others to me?

TESSA: He brought them to you? When?

BAABA: No! No! No! I went there one day, somewhere last week or last two weeks or something, I can't remember and he gave them to me. He is a nice guy you know.

TESSA: *(To herself)* I have never known this girl. She's so wicked. So, she is been seeing this Professor *(nods)* Hmmm! that is how come she got the strange 'A' in his paper. Judith was right about how she got her grades. I guess I should know better now. Each one for herself God for us all. But how can I blame her? Perhaps she is only being smart especially when they say university degrees are awarded. I don't know her to be dumb?

Or, that is what she has been doing all the time? I mean sleeping her way through school? Hmmm! I see. She, at least, gets what she wants. Of what use is my 'good girlishness'? I have been referred. I can't even have a boyfriend yet everybody knows that between the two of us, I am the good girl. If this is so, then why do the guys go after her and not me too?

It is a very strange world. My destiny, my 'dzobgeselesa'. I don't have what it takes. I don't have the heart to switch from one lie to another.

I will wait upon the Lord most high. Just like the word of God says

"Though it tarries it shall come to pass". I will find a man soon and my grades will pick up if I put in a little more effort. I will not lower my guard. The Lord will provide.

BAABA: What are you thinking about?

TESSA: Nothing. But I thought your friend Naana is dating him?

BAABA: Him who? QUIST?

TESSA: No, the Honourable.

BAABA: Oh no!

TESSA: Are you saying you are dating your friend's ex?

BAABA: Dating? No

TESSA: I don't understand this madness.

BAABA: You don't have to understand anything. You only need to know that this is not for real. I told you earlier that it is all part of exploring my campus environment. None of these is for real.

TESSA: And QUIST?

BAABA: What about him?

TESSA: Are you seeing him too?

BAABA: *(laughs to scorn)* Ohooooo! Aaaaba! Anyway, QUIST is already taken.

TESSA: By whom?

BAABA: Are you saying you don't know?

TESSA: Know what?

BAABA: Ok, I will give you the benefit of the doubt. He expressed interest, I tried to see what he is made of but I wasn't impressed so I left him for Pomaa because she was interested.

TESSA: Why was she interested?

BAABA: Grades, what else? But above that, I think the possibility of following him to America.

TESSA: Hahahahaha! Interesting. America! That girl is so much like you or better still, you are like her.

BAABA: How do you mean?

TESSA: Both of you are mothers, for Christ's sake. What kind of example do you think you are setting for your children? How on earth can any sane African woman commit to playing men with the passion both of you portray.

BAABA: Sometimes you make me feel very sad. Look at you. Look at how one broken heart has left you tattered. Look at how you are suffering because of men. You should be paying us for doing the dirty job for women like you. Do you think when our men are cheating on us and beating us, they worry about African manhood? Do you think so? Do you think that a woman is a man's slave? Do you? Do you think there is any law that restricts a woman and frees a man? The world has changed my darling. In this new era, subjugation is a choice and, freedom is a right. I claim freedom and I choose to be free from oppression. Let the men play as they always do, we too will play them to their own game. I mean to make first-class or second upper and nothing below. Trust me, by hook or crook, I will make it.

TESSA: Are you normal? What if your husband gets to know about your campus safari?

BAABA: And who says he cares? Apart from that, worst-case scenario, he will behave as he always has. *(a line of a tear falling off her eyes)* I don't even care about him anymore. In fact, I want him to hear what he made out of me. And just so you stop pitying him, his mistress has given birth to a lovely boy.

TESSA: What!

BAABA: Close that mouth your decay is showing.

TESSA: What did you just say?

BAABA: You heard me. Asabea, Kobby's mistress is pregnant.

TESSA: I thought he said he had nothing to do with her?

BAABA: I thought so too but he fooled us, right? He fooled all of us. Now you know I am not fooling myself anymore. And I won't let anybody fool me again. I have moved on and I rule my world just the way I want it.

TESSA: You don't have to destroy yourself like this just because you want to spite somebody. Remember, you can't cut your nose to spite your face.

BAABA: Destroy myself? Is that what you said? Noooo. I am having fun. I am enjoying the attention from all angles for as long as it lasts. What I am worried about now is how much I am going to miss when we vacate and I go back into that lion's den where I have to endure that monster friend of yours.

TESSA: *(she sighs)* Hmmm. It's well dear.

BAABA: It's late I have to leave now.

TESSA: *(Walking Baaba home)* My sister, sometimes I understand your pain. However, I don't think you can sustain this lifestyle for long. I suggest you talk to a counsellor. What do you think?

(Baaba does not go to her room when Tessa sees her off. she leaves for Honourable Amponsah's residence. They sit in the hall and have a conversation)

BAABA: *(knocking on the door and Honourable Amponsah grants her access)* Hi.

HON. AMPONSAH: Hello, how are you?

BAABA: *(sounding cold towards him)* Fine.

HON. AMPONSAH: Are you sure you are fine? *(no response from her)* Okay, maybe you want to drink something. *(getting her a glass of wine)* This is for you.

BAABA: *(taking the wine and placing it on the table)*

HON. AMPONSAH: Is anything wrong?

BAABA: *(not answering)*

HONOURABLE AMPONSAH: Why are you so quiet? *(After a while)* If it's about my divorce and us then I just want you to know that I will never stop loving you. You have co-operated all this while. This is the time I need you most. Baaba, I have kept my quiet on the processing of these papers because of my impending elections. The race is tough and I don't want my opponent to have me on the spot with this issue. So please, don't listen to what your friends say. Know that they are only envious of you. When all is over the divorce will sail through and you will become the MP's wife right? Just trust me I won't let you down Ok!

BAABA: *(smiling)* Are you sure?

HON. AMPONSAH: Yes. I am working fervently, just for the two of us.

BAABA: I pray so. I can't wait to be the wife of the M.P.

HON. AMPONSAH: Yes, my dear, I can't wait to have you too. Come here *(drawing her to himself, they kiss heading towards the bedroom)* You know what, let's get to the bedroom and do some sweet things to ourselves.

(After some time, Baaba making a phone call. She is talking to Kobina Esam)

BAABA: Hello *(voice reduces to whisper, turn to see if Honourable Amponsah is coming)*

KOBINA ESAN: Hello sweetheart, sorry if I woke you up.

BAABA: Come on, it is alright. How are you?

KOBINA ESAN: I miss you and I can't sleep. I thought you would come for the weekend.

BAABA: Sorry, I have some assignments to finish. Even as I am talking to you, I am working on an assignment. It's not easy but I would be free next weekend then I will visit okay.

KOBINA ESAN: Alright I will wait, please take care of yourself for me.

BAABA: Okay I will.

KOBINA ESAN: I love you.

BAABA: Me too.

KOBINA ESAN: Goodnight.

BAABA: Goodnight. *(Honourable Amponsah calls from the bedroom)* Yes dear. I am coming. I want to drink some wine, I'll be with you in a moment.

HONOURABLE AMPONSAH: Alright, please hurry and come. Ekyeaa na eedwu. *(meaning if it keeps longer, it gets cold)*

ACT 4

SCENE 1

(A day after the presidential and parliamentary elections, Tessa is now Baaba's roommate on campus, Adepa Hall Room 38, West Wing on the second floor. Entering Naana, a classmate and friend)

NAANA: Hei! Yieeeee! Hei! Yeaaa! *(Jumping about in jubilation)* Are you ladies in there?

TESSA: Come in and take a seat. How do you know the result?

NAANA: Oh! it's all over. You girls are always in the room. Come out and feel the victory.

BAABA: I am going to work on my project. The gentleman typing my work for me is lazy. I have to sit on him so that he finishes today. I will see you girls tomorrow.

TESSA: OK. Just make sure you will return with it even if it means staying overnight.

(Exit Baaba)

NAANA: Why is your friend kind of cold?

TESSA: *(Laughing with scorn)* If your husband had lost elections would you be laughing your heart out?

NAANA: Which husband?

TESSA: Honourable Amponsah of course.

NAANA: Baaba is dating Honourable Amponsah?

TESSA: That is not the only problem. She's on the verge of losing her marriage too. Now that she's gone. I'm sure he's going to find her fate with him.

NAANA: Is that man not married?

TESSA: Don't know what is wrong with Baaba anymore. She claims he is on the verge of divorce but men cannot be trusted, especially, now that he's lost the elections.

NAANA: That is true Tessa, I hear he intends joining his wife abroad and quitting his political carrier.

TESSA: Ahaaa! I said it oooo! Good Jesus Christ! Then my sister is in trouble. She was so sure that he would win and now look. Hmmm! What will happen now?

NAANA: Ah! I don't even understand you. Is this the first time a politician has lost an election?

TESSA: Hmmm! Baaba, what is she going to do?

              Kobina Esan is aware that the pregnancy she carries now is not his and that is the grounds for his divorce. Eh! What is all this? I warned herooo, I warned her but she wouldn't listen to me. Now, look at all this mess. How is she going to get out of her situation? Ah! What a disgrace! Hmmm!

NAANA: Everybody is talking about her. The only option for her now is to move off-campus for the last semester.

TESSA: The sad thing is that as for losing her marriage it is what I call a dream come true at the wrong time. The toughest blow is Honourable Amponsah joining his wife abroad instead of divorcing her.

NAANA: What does Baaba intend doing with the pregnancy?

TESSA: *(shaking her head with remorse)* I don't know. It's already three months old. The doctor says abortion is suicidal. That girl has indeed bitten more than she could chew ha!

NAANA: Oh! that is very bad. I'm sad for her.

TESSA: But it's already happened. Sometimes advice does not change a person, trials do and this is one of such.

NAANA: You are right, girl. Nevertheless, let me get going. We will talk for this later. Bye

TESSA: Bye.

ACT 4

SCENE 2

(Scene opens with a marriage dissolution meeting between Baaba and Kobina Esan in Baaba's house. They sit on opposite sides and facing each other. Each has a company of family members behind them. Their parents sit next to each other. Baaba has recovered fully and preparing to start national service. But asks her parents to disentangle her from Kobina Esan before she begins. The two families are therefore seated for this purpose. The linguist for Baaba's family rises to speak first by calling the seated to order)

LINGUIST: Agooo!

ALL: Ameeeeeee!

LINGUIST: Mese Agoooo!

ALL: Okyeame Ameee oooooh! *(deafening silence)*

LINGUIST: Yooo, thank you all for coming. On behalf of the Twedan family of Busano, Elmina, I welcome all of you to this special gathering. I would be grateful if the priest in our midst will commit this meeting into the hands of the Almighty Twediapon Nyame before we proceed.

(Baaba's younger brother, Rev. Father Abeiku Mentel Mensah, a Catholic priest of the Abease Diocese praying.

REV. FATHER: *(All rising and in an energetic and loud fashion the priest praying)* Father in heaven, we thank you for the opportunity to gather here. Your word says where two or three are gathered in your name you are present. Lord, today we are in disagreement with each other. Howbeit, we are gathered in your name. We know you to be the great arbiter that is why we cannot have a gathering like this without your presence. We, therefore, ask you, Yahweh our provider, Ebenezer, our guard, oooooh! King of Kings, God of peace and God of love *(the gathering is energized into saying amen repeatedly while Rev. Father continues praying)* Lord, we ask you to take your place in our midst. We are gathered to listen to your son and your daughter. Please Lord, let there be an understanding between them and the families gathered here. Melt every iron heart. Let your mighty presence be felt as you calm tempers and grant sound reasoning. Pour upon us your spirit of forgiveness and reconciliation. In all, grant us a fruitful deliberation even as we ask that our purpose may yield your will and yours alone. In Jesus' name, we pray, Amen. *(There is a huge roar of amen from the crowd)* In the name of the Father, the Son and the Holy Spirit *(all respond with a thundering Amen)* Shall we take our seats, please? *(all sitting. There is murmuring and smiles from both quarters in reaction to the priest's prayer)*

LINGUIST: Yoooo Osofo, thank you very much for the nicely spiced prayer. *(To the seated who are still murmuring)* Please, can we pay attention here? The Abusua Panyin of the Twidan Ebusua is ready to talk. Shall we please listen to him?

EBUSUAPANYIN: Yooo Okyeame, relay it to my own kinsmen and our guests that I wish them a hearty welcome. Let them understand that the cock that crows in the morning does not do so because it is hungry. It does so because he fears others may sleep too much. It does so to show concern. Therefore, for us to gather here like this, this morning, for me to send for our guests like this is my attempt to make sure that none of us is oversleeping. It is for me to make sure that nothing has been left too idle and too scattered to gather. Okyeame, please give everybody my Akwaaba and my warm welcome.

LINGUIST: Ebusuapanyin says
Akwaabaaaaooooo.

ALL: *(all responding)* Ye gyinodoooooooo

EBUSUAPANYIN: *(continuing)* Today, we have gathered here on a not too pleasant note. When two respectable and God-fearing families meet like this, it is the desire of all to have a pleasant reason to gather. However, since the world has not stopped rotating on its axis, the unfortunate is bound to happen at any time. We are assembled to deliberate on issues related to the marriage of our children, Esan and Baaba.

Some ten years ago, they assembled us for a much more joyous purpose. Today, they ask us to come here in mourning clothes. However, before we can start any serious deliberations, Okyeame, can we know who and who are seated here so that if there is any stranger in our midst, we can expel him before we begin our purpose for this gathering? This is a closed-circuit meeting and you should be here because you were invited.

LINGUIST: Yoooo. My brothers and sisters, at the request of the Ebusua Panyin, can we introduce ourselves so that we know who is here. As the host, we will begin with ourselves. I am Kofi Edu, the Okyeame for the Twidan Ebusua from Elmina. *(All others introducing themselves in that order including the guest family and excuses are made for those absent, noticeably, Esan's father who is on a sickbed)* Ebusua Panyin, we are done.

EBUSUA PANYIN: Please let the visitors know that this is our home but it has always been their home too since our children got married. However, because they have come to meet us here, we welcome them greatly.

LINGUIST: Yooo, our in-laws, you heard Ebusua Panyin well.

SPOKESPERSON: Yoo Okyeame, let it reach Ebusua Panyin that, as I introduced myself earlier, though I am Kwesi Twum in private, by popular request, I am the unopposed spokesperson for the Idan family of Bretua Kese also in Elmina. With permission from my people, we accept your warm welcome.

LINGUIST: *(conferring with Ebusua Panyin before speaking)* Thank you. Now, please, they say we know but we still ask. Too much meat does not spoil a soup. Therefore, our in-laws, Ebusua Panyin wants to know why you have called for this gathering this early morning.

SPOKESPERSON: *(conferring with one or two people before speaking)* Yoo, Okyeame, let Ebusua Panyin hear that we bring greetings from our people back home. We are here on a very simple but serious mission. Our daughter, Baaba, has been married to your son, Kobina Esan, for over ten years. God has blessed them with beautiful and intelligent children. We have never heard any complaints about this marriage until recently. Okyeame, Let Ebusua Panyin hear that a few weeks ago, our daughter insisted vehemently that we return the drinks you brought for her marriage to you and dissolve the marriage otherwise she will commit suicide.

ALL: eiii! Aaaarrhg! God forbids!

SPOKESPERSON: Okyeame, let Ebusua Panyin also hear that for several weeks and days we tried to listen to our daughter and also convince her to be patient for marriage is related to mileage and it connotes a long journey. In Akan, we say *Awar* meaning *Owar*. It requires patience and endurance because the journey is long. That is why during the contracting of marriage, the families of both sides are encouraged to witness and support the married. For a better support one person each from both ends are made to pledge their support to the couple so that when the storm hits, the anchors of the marriage shall hold. However, it is as though the storm that has hit Baaba and Esan's marriage has raptured the anchors that held the marriage vessel still. For months since the wrangling began, we have tried all we can as a family to do our part to keep these two together, at least for the sake of the children, but to no avail. Our persuasions have failed and here we are today to heed her call *(takes out four bottles of Schnapps)*

LINGUIST: *(Conferring with his people for a while, clearing his throat and beginning to speak)* Mr Spokesman, Okasamafo, my Ebusua Panyin would like to hear from the horse's own mouth what her reasons for opting out of this marriage are.

(Murmurings begin and continues for a while. Baaba agreeing to something rising to speak. Badua her mother looks agitated rises too. She is dragged back into her seat by Baaba's Father)

BAABA: *(she calls)* Agoo Nananom mpanyinfo.

ALL: *(they respond)* Amee.

LINGUIST: *(on his feet adjusting his cloth)* Our beautiful daughter, Ebusua Panyin wants to speak to you. Please do well to listen carefully and answer him appropriately if you have to. We are all here for the good of both of you. We too want to hear from you exactly what is chasing you out of your marriage. So that we can help both of you to make the right decision. *(Takes a seat)*

EBUSUA PANYIN: Our beautiful daughter, we are sorry that it all has to come to this but we both know that without hearing from you, what is actually driving you out of your marriage, we can do very little to give sound consent. Please tell us, does your husband starve you?

BAABA: Please No!

EBUSUA PANYIN: Does he beat you?

BAABA: *(she is quiet)*

EBUSUA PANYIN: Ewuraba Baaba, does your husband beat you?

BADUA: Are you a piece of wood? Can't you talk? Yes, he beats her. He beats my daughter. For a very long time, she has been telling me but I tell her to be patient. Look at her hands, her neck. He beats her. He has been beating my daughter. Can you even imagine that? How! How on earth can you lay your hands on her? Ask her whether

I have ever beaten her in her whole life. Then you, you, you Aaaaaaaa! *(Murmuring from both families)*

EBUSUA PANYIN: Maame Badua, please can you keep quiet and let your daughter speak for herself? We understand your anguish as a mother but as adults, we must restrain ourselves from hot-headedness in matters like this so that we can make sound judgment, so please everybody must restrain themselves. Thank you.

Auntie Baaba, I ask you the same question again, DOES YOUR HUSBAND BEAT YOU?

BAABA: Yes, he does.

ALL: Oooooh!

EBUSUA PANYIN: Hmmmm! Why do you think your husband beats you?

BAABA: Please I have no idea. He behaves as if he hates me. He yells at me, slaps me and sometimes threatens to kill me. What hurts me most is that he does these in the presence of my children. Sometimes I have the feeling that he is possessed by some marine spirit because he can be very mean. The last time he used his belt on me, I had bruises all over. Look, look at my arms, my neck and my legs. Because I am fair, for a whole month I couldn't go out otherwise people will notice that I have been physically abused.

What is it? What is it? *(Begins shedding tears)* What is it that I do not do as a wife and mother; I cook, I wash, I clean, I serve him dutifully. Even when the money he gives me is not enough, I add to it. I have never complained about what he gives out for housekeeping. He never buys me gifts but I don't complain. For all the four years that I spent in school, it is only on one occasion that he brought me some foodstuff. Thank God I have a job lest he would have starved me to death. It is because of his behaviour that I went back to school. I thought that I needed to get away for a while but believe me, his hatred for me turned worse. When he comes around, he wants to yell at me in the presence of my colleagues. Because of his behaviour whenever he says he is coming to visit me I tell him I am on my way home. Esan treats me as if I am his slave and not his wife. He teaches my children, as young as they are, to disrespect me. He even slaps me in their presence. What crime have I committed? It is not as if he is the only man in this world. There are many others who will appreciate me better. Many others who are ready to treat me with respect like a queen. Which woman here will live with a monster like him? Who here, mother or father will allow their daughter to suffer like this; ten years of battery and humiliation in this era of freedom and enlightenment? I have made my

decision. I have had it with him.
Dissolve this marriage for us so that
Esan can move on with his mistress.

WITNESSES: Eeeei!

BAABA: *(continuing)* So that he can have the
freedom to be with the woman who
can put smiles on his face and not
make him as angry as I do when he
sees me. Yes, so that he can be with
the woman he can passionately love
and make love to and not one like me
whom he treats like a whore. I am
done. I have had it with him. Please
dissolve this marriage.

EBUSUA PANYIN: Hmmmm! Our daughter,
it's ok. Wipe your tears and take a
seat. Esan, you heard the tall list
of reasons for which this beautiful
young woman you married says she
wants to quit this marriage. Kobina
Esan, our son, what is your defence
if any.

BADUA: *(Interrupting)* what defence has he, nothing. If somebody treated any of those sisters of yours like this would you be happy? Eh! Would you be happy? What defence do you have? Tell us?

LINGUIST: Maame Badua, please can you show some restraint and respect for the elders gathered here? Please.

EBUSUA PANYIN: Kobina Esan, your elders are ready to listen to you.

ESAN: Mpanyinfo, thank you for finding the time to attend this gathering. On a Saturday morning like this, the ideal thing is to take a rest after a week's hard work. Once again, thank you for coming. I also want to thank you for giving me the opportunity to tell my side of the story. It is never a pleasant thing for any man when he finds himself explaining his actions and inactions to the world regarding a woman he has duly married. Baaba is my wife. I first met her when she was in secondary school. I agreed with her parents that I was going to make sure she completed her secondary education. This I did. I do not find pleasure in recounting all that I have done for her and her family. I took care of all her expenses since she started secondary school. When she finished, her mother, Badua approached me that she preferred that I help her daughter to go through teacher training so that she can have a job. It was a laudable idea because I thought that if she had a job and earned some income, she could take care of some petty, petty expenses and also help out at home. That will also take care of some of the financial burdens I will have to carry as a man, husband and father. When she went to the training college, I was there for her. Eventually, in her final year we got married.

My elders, life has not been easy for me as a man. I pay all the bills; school fees, light bill, water bill, telephone, internet, DSTV, gas, petrol, rent, vehicle maintenance, housekeeping money, mention it, I pay. Please ask my wife what she does with her salary. Nothing. But that is not my problem. 12:00 midnight, come to my house and you will find my wife on the phone texting or speaking in such a low voice that I can't even hear what she's talking about. What kind of wife does that? I have tried to find out who the callers are and ask them to show some respect but after every call, she deletes the number. What is she hiding? Her WhatsApp chat lines are always blank but I have been hearing buzzes. Why doesn't she leave the messages on the phone? Why does she delete messages after reading? What is she hiding? What am I supposed to do when I ask her about these simple things and she has no answers for me? I told her once that I cannot accept men calling her in my presence because of the way she talks on the phone with them. One time I deleted all the phone numbers of males on her phone. Can you imagine, the next time I checked she has placed a password on the phone. That night she virtually fought me when I tried to take the phone from her. My elders, I am not surprised that today, this woman wants to quit this marriage. Of course, who wouldn't? After hopping from one man to another during her days in that university, which woman can return to her marriage? Who says I am not aware of the pregnancies she aborted?

(murmuring from witnesses) Who says I am not aware that in addition to other men she sees women too? Who could be possessed here? Me or her? I knew this day would come. I have been ready for it. Ask her when last I touched her as my wife. It is about a year ago. I don't know what disease I could catch. Ask her when last I ate

her food or ask her to do anything for me or even call her. She has enough calls from more important people. She doesn't need me. And I don't need her. The mother of my children must be a good example for them. They are watching her and everything she does. I fear they would become like her that is why I also agree that this marriage is dissolved if she does not see anything wrong with her attitude, if she is not ready to change, please take the drinks and let her go. *(All quiet)*

EBUSUA PANYIN: Our son, we have heard you. Please take your seat. Our daughter, do you have anything to say concerning the allegations levelled against you by your husband?

BAABA: *(rising to her feet)* My elders, I refrain from commenting on what Esan here has said about me. I appreciate all the help he gave me while I was growing up. However, if he mistreats me because he spent so much on me, then he has made a grave mistake. If he kept surfing my phone and pestered me with who I speak to because he did not trust me then that is the more reason why the two of us must go our separate ways. As for the children, they are mine too as much as they are his. He cannot prevent me from seeing them. If he extends his mistreatment to them, he will have me and my wrath to contend with. I will, therefore, pray that my people waste no more time but return the engagement drinks as a sign of annulment of this marriage between us. Thank you

EBUSUA PANYIN: Okyeame.

LINGUIST: LINGUIST: Ebusua Panyin.

EBUSUA PANYIN: Let both parties know that we have heard them. They are adults. They have deliberated on this matter for long and have come to their conclusions. However, as divorce is not a pleasant thing for any family, Okyeame, please ask the couple for the last time whether they still insist on their decision to annul this marriage.

LINGUIST: My lady and my gentleman here, in fact, Mr and Mrs., you heard what Ebusua Payin said. Are you both sure about this decision of yours to end this marriage? You, our daughter, first answer the elders.

BAABA: Yes, my elders. There is no way I want to have anything called marriage to do with this man. He is a wife beater.

LINGUIST: Hmmm. Yoooo. Eehhh how about you our son? Are you sure about your decision to accept the drinks your wife and her people have returned? Ebusua Panyin wants to know whether you still want him to accept them.

KOBINA ESAN: Okyeame: Please tell my elders to go ahead and accept them.

126

EBUSUA PANYIN: Alright. This is a very sad day. All the same, you can only force the Carmel to the river, you can in no way force it to drink from it. It is unfortunate that this once beautiful marriage has come to this sad end. Okyeame, let the other family know that they are free to present the brink of dissolution.

BAABA'S UNCLE: *(presenting four bottles of schnapps to Okyeame)* Here you go Okyeame.

EBUSUA PANYIN: Thank you. We all know that there are children involved here. Please, it is late now. We have been sitting for hours. The sun is about to set. Please let the two, father and mother of the children, come over tomorrow and finish with arrangement regarding co-parenting and custody of the children. This ends our agenda for the day. Please if Osofo is still with us, pray and thank God for our gathering.

OSOFO: Dear God, we thank you for today's deliberations. Your word tells us to give thanks to you in all things. This is why we are grateful for your presence. May the decisions we have taken here serve the best of humanity. Please grant us all a safe journey back home in Jesus' name we pray amen. In the name of the Father, the Son and the Holy Spirit Amen. *(All responding, Amen)*

ACT 5

SCENE 1

(Scene opening with Baaba making a phone call. She is sitting in the staff room of her school in the next town, where she is having her national service.)

BAABA: Hello, Eeeiii! Tessa, Sofo Maame, how are you doing?

TESSA: Very fine and you?

BAABA: I am fine. I haven't heard from you in a while.

TESSA: You don't call me, I call all the time. If I hadn't called today you would never have called. I guess you have special people that you call and I am not one of them.

BAABA: *(laughing)* Oh ho! Please don't say that. I will call you, promise. What is going on at your end?

TESSA: Nothing much. Just trying to settle in. I have been given the first-year class but they are yet to report so, for now, I am just reading around their syllabus. You know service persons are mere adjuncts. We only follow instructions and follow the crowd. What about you?

BAABA: It's the same with me. I guess because we are new to the senior high school curriculum, and also because we are doing national service, all the schools prefer, we start with the first years. I am also waiting for them to report. I hear their reporting date is the 25th of this month. I like the weather here. It is cool and less polluted. Above all, I like the peace of mind. I guess it is time to pause for some introspection. My brother calls it stock-taking, regrouping or re-strategizing.

TESSA: *(laughing)* I was waiting for you to add that. I prefer the last term. We both need re-strategizing after all that we have been through on campus. The important thing is that if you are happy there, then that is a good thing. Just take care of yourself as you prepare to give yourself a fresh start.

BAABA: You are so right. It has been a very murky and muddling last four years. But I don't regret all the experiences. They are life lessons that do not come on the silver platter.

TESSA: You are very brave, my sister. Very, very, brave

BAABA: (*Laughing*) You always say that.

TESSA: Yes, you are and I learnt a lot from you. If you fear to live, you live to die. Look at me? I don't like this, I don't like that, he doesn't go to church, I am a deaconess, he doesn't have a good job, he is this and not that. Look at me. Forty-three years and counting.

BAABA: You see, the problem with is that you say very negative things about yourself. Remember, life and death are in the power of the tongue. Wish yourself well. Believe that at the appointed time the right man will come around. If you had been in my circles, like Naana, I would ask you to find a decent man and have a couple of children with him. If it works out, fine. If it doesn't, you can afford to take care of your children and let him be.

TESSA: Nononononono, that is not possible. I am a deaconess in the Pentecost Church. I am also the leader of the Righteous Women's Fellowship. How can I get pregnant without not being married first?

BAABA: That is what I refer to as circles. In your case. You must increase your faith in the Lord and trust him to show up as he did for Job.

TESSA: Exactly! That your friend, Naana, do you hear from her?

BAABA: Not really. The last time we spoke was when she complained bitterly about how you had passed an unpleasant comment about her boyfriend.

TESSA: Oh! What did I say, I only said, she should stop taking the gentleman's money because there is no way her Jehovah Witness society will agree to her marriage to him? Everybody can see that the man loves her but she doesn't love him. She is your friend. You should talk to her.

BAABA: Noooo! I like to mind my own business sister. She is very angry with you though!

TESSA: Me? And not you? I don't care anyway. If you had done that, she would have said it and even peddle it all over the world. She can go to the Ganges for all I care.

BAABA: Because of that she has been quite distant from me but I just want her to be. I have more important things to worry about.

TESSA: She has never been my friend, you know? She was your friend. I only entertained her because of you. Does she know about you and Honourable Amponsah?

BAABA: *(laughing aloud)* Don't worry about that. Is she not the one who introduced us? Is she not the very one who gave me his card and said he wanted me to call him? Did Naana say she had plans to become a second wife to him? She can go to hell. She even knows my Dad had him jailed once upon a time. It was a game and it is over. She can go back to him. None of my business

TESSA: How are my children doing?

BAABA: They are fine. They are with their dad. I allowed him to keep them so that their schooling is not interrupted. They are fine. You know they have been through a lot. They struggled to cope with all the divorce drama and for myself, I have struggled with the presence of mind to face the public after all that happened. Everybody thought I was to blame. Nobody considered the pain and suffering I had to endure in that marriage for many years.

TESSA: It is a very sad situation. I still can't believe that Kobby did all those horrible things to you.

BAABA: You know, on the day I packed out, the kids came to me and asked why I cheated on their father.

TESSA: What! Where did they get that from?

BAABA: Poison. That is what I call it. He had schooled these little ones to think that I was a bad woman and a bad mother. They see me as irresponsible and unfaithful that is why their father always beats me *(choking with tears. blowing her wet nose)*

TESSA: Why would he do a thing like that?

BAABA: He hates me. He has hated me from the first day we got married. He hated me because I was unwilling to marry him. He thinks I embarrassed him by initially preferring to abort the pregnancy instead of marrying him. He thinks that I made him a laughing stock especially because many women had been dying to date him but I treated him with disdain with my refusal to marry him. But I don't blame him. I blame my father. He wouldn't listen to me. He too was thinking about his image in church. What would they say? The father of a priest and the catechist who has been teaching other children to do the right thing has her own daughter pregnant out of wedlock. This is what he was worried about and not my welfare.

TESSA: I'm sorry my sister, that you had to go through all these. How did you combine this with your studies?

BAABA: You of all people do not need to ask. I call it ways and means. The latter days were quite messy but I am grateful to God for the second chance. I learnt my lessons the hard way. That last clearance nearly killed me. Come to think of it, who told Kobby about it?

TESSA: Surely not I.

BAABA: Do I even care? At least, the time I spent on the hospital bed was worth it. I got the peace of mind to think my life through. It enabled me to summon the courage to take control of my life.

TESSA: That was a brave move.

BAABA: Yes. The threat of suicide did the trick. It was not as if I did not mean it, though. I just couldn't believe that it worked. If only I had known that this was all it took to reach the gates of freedom, I would have taken it long ago.

TESSA: You really meant it when you said you wanted to be Ama Atta Aidoo's Esi.

BAABA: *(Laughing)* Hahahahahaa. Do you remember all that? I meant every word I said? I was tired of marital slavery. Worse of all I was tired of feeling trapped and helpless. That was not the life I wanted or even imagined for myself. T, every woman wants to be loved and respected not beaten like a drum and humiliated. What happened to all the romance, the love and the care that we read about in *Romeo and Juliet?*

TESSA: I guess those are fiction and that is what they will remain. True love does not exist. Not in marriage. Look at me. The same fear of being ridiculed and humiliated in church as the leader of the women's fellowship. The men are not coming and I am ageing. I wish I even had a child but now how can I have one out of wedlock? How?

BAABA: But what about Ken? I think he will be a good husband.

TESSA: Which Ken?

BAABA: Which Ken? Or is he not called Ken? Your sister's schoolmate. I pray that he lives up to the bill when you settle down.

TESSA: Too late. You should have prayed when we were dating.

BAABA: How do you mean?

TESSA: I have nobody to talk to so I just cry and then go back to sleep. I try to find some comfort in my wet pillow.

BAABA: Oh no! Not you. What is the problem? Is it because you refused to have sex before marriage?

TESSA: Sex?

BAABA: So, what was the problem?

TESSA: Ken is married.

BAABA: Oh! The marriage happened and you didn't tell me?

TESSA: *(laughing)* One-month marriage. How could I share the news with anybody? We had the engagement with plans for marriage the next. Only to learn that he was married to another woman in Belgium?

BAABA: Marriage for convenience?

TESSA: I hear he is now in prison because the woman found out about us and reported him to the police so they incarcerated him when he went back. For five years since he left after our honeymoon, I have not set eyes on him. I only hear his voice when he calls. Initially, he told me he has network problems in his house. He also said he can't make calls at work. This means I only hear from him when he calls. This has been the situation for the past five years.

BAABA: Good Jesus! How are you coping with this?

TESSA: You are married to a Muslim and you are saying Jesus *(both laughing)*

BAABA: Yussif is a human being. Answer my question.

TESSA: There is nothing to answer. I find myself in this cage called marriage. I don't even have the keys to open and flee. This is a registered marriage. Divorce requires consent from both parties. My pastor thinks I should be patient. He keeps reminding me of the need to pray as prayer moves mountains. Sometimes I feel I have no options but to stay put. I am the president of the Regional Women's Fellowship and the Regional Counselling Cohort. How do I explain this to the world? Is it that I have no faith in God's power to turn the situation around or what? What will be my reason for calling it quit? Do

I begin to accept that marriage is not meant for me? Worse case, I haven't even had any man look my way or take a stir let alone try to propose. This is not as though I could gunner the courage to say yes when I am supposed to be supposedly married.

BAABA: Don't say that. Think positively. Life and death are in the power of the tongue.

TESSA: Hmmmm! What are you now? A pastor?

BAABA: Not really but I know how you feel. I know you, Sis.

TESSA: But for how long can I continue to live like this. I am even asking him to come home so that we can annul this marriage then I will know that I am single and then he too can focus on his woman. I have always prayed to be able to settle down and have my own family but this is not the way I want it. I am not sure this answer came from God. Could God be testing me or what? As I speak, the last time I heard from him was three months ago.

BAABA: And what did he say?

TESSA: Nothing.

BAABA: Nothing? What do you mean by nothing? How could he not say anything?

TESSA: I don't know anything anymore *(breaking down in tears)*

BAABA: Does he send you money for upkeep.

TESSA: That is if he was keeping anything at all. It looks as if I don't exist in his world. I want to believe it is only when he sees somebody who looks like me that he remembers that in the other world of his, there is a woman he is supposed to be married to. *(Shaking head in disbelief)* I am not sure God really heard what I asked for otherwise, he would not have sent me this monster to bruise my wounds.

BAABA: Oh no! Please, Tess, you have to be strong. You have to be strong. Breaking down and feeling this dejected is not good for your situation. Please, Tess, I need you to be strong until we can find a way out.

TESSA: I hear you, my sister. It is late, 2 pm already. I think you have to go now. You promised to call so keep that promise and take care.

BAABA: Haaahahaha I hear you. I even have a class so we will talk later. Take care too and remember that there is always a way out.

TESSA: Ok bye.

BAABA: Bye

ACT 5

SCENE 2

(In school, Baaba's sitting alone behind her table recapping her own life experiences. She has a pile of students' exercise books on a writing desk standing near her table. It is a five-minute walk away from the first-year classroom block. Her class with Form One C for the day on Characterization in Ama Atta Aidoo's "Anowa" is about thirty minutes away)

BAABA: *(speaking aloud to herself in her room)* Freedom at last. It's good to have some peace of mind. Finally, no yelling, no slapping, no kicking in the tummy, no arguments, no humiliation *(wipes tears)* I get to start all over. And this Saani guy, he surely is a big risk. Why is he a big risk? That's Naana's boyfriend you know? Correction, ex-boyfriend. Yes, ex-boyfriend. Very true. And why can't I date her ex-boyfriend? Is she my sister? Even if she is so what? In this case, she is just a friend. Friend? Correction, acquaintance. True, very true, acquaintance. But he is not as handsome as I wished. Hahahaha. Do you prefer a handsome man who will maltreat you? Surely no. I won't... But he is not bad? Most men are not handsome anyway. Yesooo, like ODUM. Hahahaa ODUM too. Hmmm! Great expedition. Where? The campus of cause. I had fun though. I also got to know exactly what I want. And what was that? Love? It is real. It exists and I think I can find it in this Muslim. Do I have to become a Muslim? Nope. Muslim men can marry outside their religion. Hassan's wife is not a Muslim and she is happy. So I can marry him. He is an American citizen. Big bonus. My dream of living in America is finally here. I hope the embassy doesn't give me problems as they do to others. I wasted all that money trying to link up with that boy in this same America. One thousand Ghana cedis in all. Anyway, no pain no gain. How about children? One or two shouldn't be bad. Preferably two boys. That will make two boys and two girls. I should have them in America. America! America! Great country. Finally, I will live there. I can't imagine all the nice clothes and shoes and bags and high-class fashion and he is ready to pay. I will go back to school. I will try the Journalism school there. The exam in Ghana was too difficult. I always knew I wasn't going to pass. America will be easier. My experience in the Ghana exam and a little more effort should see me through successful. Water will find its own level. The most important thing is that I am free and I am on track for a fresh start.

(A student entering but she does not see her because she is caught in her thoughts. She is stunned) What do you want?

STUDENT: Madam, please it is 2:30 pm and we have a class with you.

BAABA: Alright. I have forgotten your name.

STUDENT: Madam please I am Ewuresi Hanson.

BAABA: Yes Ewura. Send these books to your class. I will be there soon.

STUDENT: Yes Madam. *(She takes the books away and Baaba goes to the class soon)*

ACT 5

SCENE 3

(Scene opens in the room of Saani. Baaba has relocated to the United States of America. She lives in the States with his new husband, Saani. Tessa calls her from Ghana to check up on her. Tessa is in her sitting room)

BAABA: Hello.

TESSA: Hello, did I interrupt anything? I thought I heard some background noise.

BAABA: You are crazy no.

TESSA: You sound tired.

BAABA: It's very cold this evening. I am just feeling a bit lazy.

TESSA: It's quite cold here too.

BAABA: How are you doing?

TESSA: Great.

BAABA: Great!

TESSA: Yes Great.

BAABA: Hmmm, you want to tell me about it? You sound super excited.

TESSA: Hahahaaha.   Maybe I sound stronger now.

BAABA: So tell me how you did it.

TESSA: Easily! Just went back to school.

BAABA: And?

TESSA: Got busy.

BAABA: Good but how?

TESSA: Back to school for my masters.

BAABA: Oh! Congratulations! Now that is my girl. Remember how we always blamed Mara for allowing Akobi to abuse her?

TESSA: Yeah.

BAABA: Good. That is where I derived my strength. The lesson is simple. You have your life to lead. You don't have to allow another woman's spoilt son to make you miserable. Look at you. Oh my God! I am so happy for you.

TESSA: Hahahaha. I am happy too. It took me forever to realize that the bond of 1844 includes my own emancipation. I feel like the whole world has been lifted off my shoulders. Oh God! Thank you anyway.

BAABA: I can tell. Is there anything I am missing?

TESSA: *(laughs aloud)* So much my dear.

BAABA: Really!

TESSA: I am due next month

BAABA: Due to what?

TESSA: My first child.

BAABA: What! Wow! Wow! Wow!

TESSA: Yes.

BAABA: And who is that lucky fellow?

TESSA: George.

BAABA: Do I know him?

TESSA: Don't think so.

BAABA: Congrats dear but you have to tell me more about this.

TESSA: Ok so we met on campus. We are course mates.

BAABA: Where? Which campus?

TESSA: The University of Education, Winneba.

BAABA: Ahhh! That should be when you started your masters?

TESSA: Yep.

BAABA: Ooooooh! I see. Ok and then?

TESSA: In fact, we are study mates.

BAABA: Hehehehe, fast connection thatooo.

TESSA: Hahaha you are right. I picked a few lessons from you right.

BAABA: Ahaaa! I always tell you, each one for himself, God for us all. If you want it just go for it. Ah! What is man? Whatever you do, somebody will talk about it. Happy yourself my sister. Ehe, so what happened next?

TESSA: You are right oo. Some of us are just dull. We are so afraid of what others will say.

BAABA: So how did you grab this one sis?

TESSA: How? I used my eyes and my smiles.

BAABA: Hahahahaha. It's electric bugi bugi. Woow!

TESSA: When he is talking, I stare into his face like a moron but immediately I catch his eye, I give him a wide shy smile and turn away. I did this for several weeks until one day he held my hand and squeezed it. Then I knew I was there.

BAABA: Hahahahaa. Magical sentimentality magic. Wow!

TESSA: Then the messages started, then the calls followed and then the visit happened. After about three visits we had moved from kisses to heaven. Just after one trip to the moon, he proposed marriage. Then I found out a month later that I was four weeks pregnant.

BAABA: Haahahahaa. Sharp, sharp. Thank God. And Mr...?

TESSA: He granted the divorce finally when I told him about George.

BAABA: Just like that?

TESSA: Yes. He even apologized for wasting my time and wished me well. He came down himself to finalize the divorce. Can you imagine?

BAABA: He is a man of conscience. He knows what he was doing was not right. If somebody had done that to his sister, he surely would not have liked it.

TESSA: Hmmm. So we had a simple traditional marriage and then went to the court to sign. No big ceremonies and we are fine.

BAABA: Thank God. See, I told you. We have more power in this world as women than we ever assume. If only we can muster the courage to make bold decisions and carry them out life would be far better than what we have no. No more moralises.

TESSA: Hahahhaha a new disease for the scientists to research into.

BAABA: They have to consult us

TESSA: Do you check on the kids and their father?

BAABA: Interesting question. Anyway, the kids but not necessarily their father.

They are fine. I spoke to them only yesterday. School reopens on Monday so I sent them some school supplies. I wanted them to come over for the summer holidays but their father refused.

TESSA: Why?

BAABA: Maybe he thinks I would not let them go back.

TESSA: Oh please!

BAABA: Yes, but I am patient. In two years they will be eighteen and nineteen and old enough to make a decision, according to the court. Then they can decide to come and he can't stop them.

TESSA: Has he married that lady?

BAABA: Good you asked. When I once asked you that do you know what he does in my absence you told me I was a quarrel mongrel. See? He married the very lady I always complained about.

TESSA: Hmmm! Some men! He has a child with her right?

BAABA: Yes they have two now.

TESSA: Does the lady treat your kids well?

BAABA: I guess so. They haven't complained yet though. And mum hasn't said anything about this yet so I guess they are fine. Besides, they in the boarding house. They come home briefly during vacation. They like to spend time with my mum. That also helps. It is not the best situation I wanted for them but I am helpless at least for now. Hopefully, all will work out well pretty soon.

TESSA: Insha Allah!

BAABA: Exactly. God indeed has kept us through it all. We have gone through the good, the bad and the ugly. Thank you, Tessa, you have been that good friend who has seen me through it all. God bless you.

TESSA: God bless you too. You inspire me a lot.

BAABA: Amen. As I said last month, I will be in Ghana by the weekend for my dad's funeral.

TESSA: Yes. Time flies. I will pick you up at the airport. Send me your flight itinerary.

BAABA: Very well. We do the catching up when we meet. Good morning

TESSA: Good morning dear.

THE END

Made in the USA
Middletown, DE
31 March 2022